Curvy Girl Magic

ISBN:

Cover Design by Francis Ho
Interior Design: Antoinette Johnson
Editor: Elizabeth Goran

Style Inspiration

And one day she discovered that she was fierce, and strong and full of fire, and that not even she could hold herself back because her passion burns brighter than her fears.

-Mark Anthony

#Curvygirlmagic

Introduction

Hey loves, I am so glad you decided to pick up this book and be inspired by the style in it. You have no idea how excited I am that somehow, the universe (or faith) has brought this book into your lap. When writing this book, I only had one thing on my mind, and that was to create a book that showcases plus-size fashion to everyone, while also giving you style inspiration for your everyday life. I noticed that there were not a lot of styling books for curvy women, and it gave me the idea to create one, based on your favorite bloggers and influencers. I had so much fun writing this book, and I hope you have as much fun reading it. I want you to be able to use #CurvyGirlMagic to release that inner magic in you, to be comfortable, and most importantly to feel completely confident in what you are wearing. This book will give you style inspiration, tips, and shopping guides to find the perfect plus-size clothing store for you, no matter where you are in the world. When reading this book, I hope you realize how beautiful you are and love yourself, be confident, and always stay true to yourself.

Antoinette J

The Sexiest
Thing About
A Women
is Her
Hustle.

-Unknown

#Currygirlmagic

Bossbabe

This is for all my Girl Bosses, who are making money moves and building their empire from either the comfort of their home, or in an office with their team. If you are working for a small business or work at a place with a casual dress code, figure out exactly what is acceptable to wear during your day at work. Instead of wearing a business suit, you could switch it up to jeans or khakis, flat shoes, and a casual blouse, and depending on your workplace, you may also be able to wear sneakers and a t-shirt. Always make sure to be neat and professional, no matter what you wear.

Viv N
Heartprintandstyle.com
@heartprintandstyle

When you are dressing business professional, you have to look like a boss. However, business professional is not exactly business formal, where you must break out your best shoes and suit. If your company has that strict of a dress code, you can wear a dress shirt and pant suit with heels, with a blazer to complete the look.

Nicole V
Stylevicksen.com
@stylevicksen

For the girls who work in an office space, some of you may usually be wearing business casual. This is great because you do not have to wear suits every day, however this does not mean that you can wear very casual pieces like jeans and a sweater. Having a dress shirt, collared shirt, and dress pants in your wardrobe is essential.

Sara .S
Theprepgal.com
@Theprepgal

One is never

overdress or

undressed

with a Little

Black

Dress.

- Karl Lagerfeld

#LBD

Emma. H
Emmahillstyling.com
@Emmatamsinhill

Every girl always has a little black dress in their closet, whether it is for a night out, or just for an everyday look. It is a classic, a staple in your wardrobe. If you ask any of your girlfriends if they have one, I guarantee they will say yes. You can also go for a sexier look with the LBD by wearing a bodycon style, similar to how Emma Hill does, paired with heels. This look is fantastic for going out with your friends or for a date with your partner.

The LBD is the perfect piece when you have nothing to wear going out. This design is a win because you can style it any way you want (i.e. edgy, trendy, sexy) and you will still look amazing in it. Sarah Chiwaya has an amazing outfit comprised of a fitted LBD with black boots.

Sarah. C
CurvilyFashion.com
@curvily

Cinderella never asked for a prince she asked for a night out and a dress

- Unknown

#Curvygirlmagic

Girls Night Out

When having a girls' night out, date night, or just enjoying nightlife, there are a lot of options that you can go with for the perfect look. If you are going for a conservative, yet sexy style, Telisha from The Fashionable Traveler pairs a purple dress with cheetah print heels.

Telisha. R
Fashionabletraveler.com
@Thefashionabletraveler

If you are going for more of a trendy look, this all-white outfit slayed by Sasha Ruddock of Flaw of Couture gives a sexy vibe for going out on the town. If you are all about wanting to feel like the sexiest person in the room, then you can try out key fabrics like silk or latex which instantly give you sex appeal, without showing much. You can also try different styles like a bodycon (which shows off your curves) like Emma Hill did on page 15, or you can try a jumpsuit or a two-piece set.

Sasha. R
Focapparel.storenvy.com
@Flawsofcouture

Each
Moment of
the Year
Has it Own
Beauty.

- Uknown

#Currygirlmagic

Season

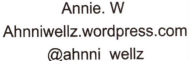

Annie. W
Ahnniwellz.wordpress.com
@ahnni_wellz

Spring is the hardest season to dress for, as you are transitioning from extreme cold weather to mild warm weather, so finding the perfect outfit can be difficult. When searching for an outfit, it can be hard to find pieces that can make due. Some days, you may have to wear a jacket and long sleeves, while other days, the weather may be appropriate enough to wear a t-shirt and shorts. Denim on denim is the perfect combo for everyday styles, as you can wear it all season, and in spring, you can really make the jean combo stand out. Style blogger Ahnni Wellz does the perfect denim on denim look, just in time for spring.

The sun is finally out, and it is time to go out with your bestie to brunch, the beach, and amazing parties. The maxi dress is the perfect summer look, as it flows beautifully. You can wear shorts during the summer, or go with the maxi dress like plus-size model Ashleigh, who is rocking this blue maxi.

Ashleigh. D
Patreon.com/AshleighDunn
@Ashleigh_dunn

The leaves are falling off the trees, and the weather is starting to get a bit chilly, so it is time to bust out your sweaters and your new fall booties so you can stroll with your family and friends in this colorful transition.

Megan. F
@Mmmeganfisher

This season is perfect for bundling up in your favorite jackets, sweaters, and winter booties. Winter is about looking stylish, but at the same time being warm, because winter can be very brutal depending on where you are. A stylish winter coat with tall boots is the perfect combination for the cold.

Blair
Notebalir.com
@Noteblair

Life isn't
Perfect But
your Outfit
Can be.

- Unknown

#Curvygirlmagic

Causal Slay

While there are days where you dress up and slay the world, there are also days when you just want to kick back and relax. Your outfit can reflect the kind of day which you are having. You can always look good in a causal style, like blogger Brianna McDowell from The B Word in her basic long sleeve, skirt, and sneakers.

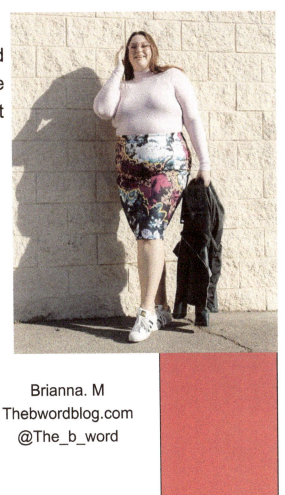

Brianna. M
Thebwordblog.com
@The_b_word

If your going out on a causal location with your bestie, it's always good to dress it up a little bit with heels like the style bloggers Kruves of Steels are doing.

Florence & Nyonyozi
Kruvesofsteels.com
@Kruvesofsteels

And I said to my body softly I want to be your Friend. It took a long breath and replied I have been waiting a long time for this.

-Unknown

#Currygirlmagic

Bay Watch

Sandae
Curvygirlontherun,blogspot.com
@Curvygirlontherun

When the sun is boiling hot, and you want to go swimming or go to the beach with your friends, a bathing suit can bring you confidence and keep you cool for the summer season. Sandae from Curvy Girls on the Run gives us a taste of the perfect swimwear look in her bikini during a fun day at the beach.

If you are into a sexier swim look, a monokini is a full piece bathing suit with high sex appeal. Fashion blogger Antoinette Johnson is rocking a red monokini in a beautiful tropical destination.

Workout because you love your body not hate it.

-Unknown

#Curvygirlmagic

Let's Workout

As the healthy lifestyle takes over the world, plus-size women all over have been loving their body and getting into shape physically and mentally. Working out can help your body detox from all the stress that you have, and the feeling after a hour at the gym can really make a difference in your day to day life. This plus-size blogger looks amazing in her workout clothes, and is creating a positive atmosphere for herself.

Tessenie. M
Tesseniemowatt.com
@Tesseniemowatt

Shape Guide

Busty

The busty woman has a larger measurement across her chest. Her hips and midsection may be curvy, but are usually slimmer than her chest area. A V-neck is flattering for those with a busty shape. Even for those with lots of cleavage, a small V-neck can help elongate your neckline and make your top half look smaller. A high neckline, like a turtleneck, will bring attention to the busty frame.

Tangeia. S
@Cheif_Tan

Pear

The pear shape is very similar to an hourglass shape, but the bust and waist are smaller compared to larger hips and thighs. Finding jeans will be difficult as your waist can be a size 14 while your hips are a size 16, which is why I recommend getting jeans specifically made for curvy women. Plus-size clothing brand Addition Elle carries jeans that are specifically for women with a small waist and big hips, called their curvy fit.

Sililroj. A
@Nancy_kakkara

Rectangle

The rectangle is the straight body type, where just like a ruler, there are no distinct curves between the hips, waist, and bust. A shift dress is great in order to give your body more dimension, and a statement necklace will garner attention. If you want to keep your straight frame, wearing boyfriend jeans will help to create that shape.

Carla. D
@Carlasaurus

Other Shapes...

Hourglass

Those with the hourglass body shape have full hips and busts with a slimmer stomach. Beside the pear body shape, this is the most common body shape that plus-size women have. Bodycon dresses are flattering to highlight the curves, and are perfect for every occasion. Also, a peplum top with a flared waist will help keep your waistline proportionate with your hips.

Apple

Those with an apple body shape have a wider measurement in the middle, while their legs, shoulders, and hips are smaller in proportion. A tunic top is perfect to flatter the middle, and give your body an hourglass shape. A short sheath dress is also good, because its straight cut plays your proportions down, while the short hemline gives attention to your legs.

Acknowledgement

This book holds a special place in my heart, as I combined my two passions for writing and fashion, and created something beautiful. This is for all the people who believe in me, who told me I can do anything once I set my mind to it. I want to thank you all for helping me realize that I can do anything I love. To my mom, who told me I can be whoever I want to be, and to my sisters for being my biggest cheerleaders, and also pushing me to do and be better. This book could not have happened without an amazing person who kept pushing me to write a book because he knew I always wanted to, and was there for me in the beginning stages when I needed it the most. Bubba, thank you for being the fuel for me to write this, and for helping me to start to create something that I did not know I would fall in love with. And lastly, thank you to the plus-size community for inspiring me to create this style guide. All you fashionable ladies encouraged me in every way with your personalities and styles to create this, so thank you.

Plus Size Directory

These are all the shops that I reccomend to all my curvy babes for the most stylish looks

1. Additional Elle (www.additionelle.com)
2. Penningtons (www.penningtons.com)
3. Sexyplus Clothing (www.sexyplusclothing.com)
4. Volutuous Inc. (www.voluptuouscothing.com)
5. Your Big Sister Closet (www.yourbigsistercloset.com)
6. Gussied Up (www.gussiedup.ca)
7. Fashion Nova (www.fashionnova.com)
8. Lane Byrant (www.lanebryant.com)
9. By Ashley Stewart (www.byashleystewart.com)
10. Posh Shoppe (www.iheartposhshoppe.com)
11. Asos (www.asos.com)
12. Forever 21 (www.forever21.com)
13. Torrid (www.torrid.com)
14. Boohoo (www.boohoo.com)
15. Pretty Little Thing (www.prettylittlething.com)
16. Missguided (www.missguided.us)

17. Swimsuit for All (www.swimsuitforall.com)

18. Premme (www.premme.us)

19. Old Navy (www.oldnavy.com)

20. Rebdolls (www.rebdolls.com

21. Rue21 (www.rue21.com)

22. Charlotte Russe (www.Charlotterusse.com)

23. Eloqui (www.eloqui.com)

24. GS Love (www.gslovesme.com)

25. Debshop (www.debshop.com)

26. Shop FOC Apparel
(www.shopfocapparel.com)

27. Monfi C (www.monfic.com)

28. Everything Chic and Curvy

29. Stylish Apparel (www.stylishapparelco.com)

30. Pheline Couture

15. River Island (www.riverisland.com)

16. Eleven60 (www.myeleven60.com)

17. Chic and Curvy Boutique

18. Curve culture boutique

19. Fashion to Figures
(www.nyandcompany.com/fashion-to-figure/)

20. Elomi Lingerie (www.elomilingerie.com)

21. Curvy Sense (www.curvysense.com)

Shout out to all the girls working on loving there bodies

Cause that shits hard and I am so proud of you!!

About the Authour

Antoinette Johnson became fascinated with fashion and body positivity during the rise of social media. After starting her blog, sShe notice how hard it was to find stylish clothing for plus size women and starting finding brands that have trendy items for curvy women and would write about it in her blog.

Antoinette is the founder and CEO of Cocktails with Antoinette which is a body positivity event to help women find confidence through fashion and conversation that she has yearly and is also uses her love for fashion as a personal/fashion stylist.

Beside being a overall #Girlboss Antoinette attend College and is getting her degree in Fashion Managment.

Instagram: @_antoinettejohnson
Facebook: @antoinettejohnsonc1
Twitter: @_antoinettejohn
Snapchat: @beyondtruth_o
Website: www.antoinetttejohnson.weebly.com

www.ingramcontent.com/pod-product-compliance
Lightning Source LLC
Chambersburg PA
CBHW041635050326
40689CB00024B/4965